Divine Essays
from the Spirit Within

Divine Essays
from the Spirit Within

By

Darryl Williams

ISBN: 0-7596-0131-3

This book is printed on acid free paper.

1stBooks - rev. 02/21/02

ACKNOWLEDGMENTS

I have to first thank the divine for ALL.

The process of working on this book could not of been done without the support and cooperation of some very important people. I want to thank my two sons Justin and Delvon and my mother Linda for allowing me to have some quiet and free time.

I also want to thank my brothers and sisters by choice Junior, Lesia, Robin, Raymond and Tony. Also a special thanks to Abdul, Wade and Mark (I wish you peace), Cemeco and Sharron. There are many more that I want to say thank you to and you know who you are.

CONTENTS

THE CONCEPT

One evening I went to bed at my usual time. I was having a normal sleep when on this particular night I was awakened by the spirit. I thought at first that I was just having a bad dream so I rolled over to go back to sleep. I soon realized that I was not dreaming but that the spirit was talking to me. I started to pay very close attention once I realized what was happening. The spirit was giving me the framework for this book. All the information I got was very general. The spirit did not give me any great details though. When my talk with the spirit was over I was very frustrated because I really wanted to know more. I wanted step by step instructions on how I was going to go about starting this book. I did not get my wish though. The spirit gave me just enough to get started and the rest was left up to me.

After trying unsuccessfully to go back to sleep I got out of bed and went to the computer to see what I could write. It was at that very moment that I wondered if I was up to doing what the spirit wanted me to do. I knew that I had many magical and mystical experiences during the course of my spiritual journey so far. I had also done a lot of reading on spirituality, religion and self awareness over the last few years. I searched my mind trying to recall things that I had read to give myself a starting point but nothing came from that effort. I closed my eyes and prayer for guidance. My prayer was answered in the form of extreme peace.

It was in that peace that I soon realized that I already had a starting point. I had seen, witnessed and experienced many wonderful things as I have moved along on my journey to spiritual freedom. This knowledge was a very powerful acknowledgment for me. I knew that I had my own stories of spiritual enlightenment and personal relationship with the spirits to share. I knew I had to write about my own personal experiences with the spirit.

My only concern at this point was did I have the patience that would be necessary to see this work to the very end. Patience is one of the areas in my life that I constantly have to work on.

The essays that I have written are broken into two sections. In the first section I talk about the fundamentals or as I have titled them the "Principal of life". The next section is titled "Inspirations". It is a collection my own motivational readings. All of which have been essential to me on my road to true spiritual clarity. The one thing that all of my essays have in common are that they are all very personal and represent different periods of personal and spiritual growth in my life.

The Principals of life that I write about have always come up in every thing that I have seen, heard or experienced on my journey to becoming and remaining spiritually intact. After becoming spiritually aware, I realized that the truth of all the principals of life are unchanging. The truth of what they are today is the same as it had been yesterday and this truth will be the same tomorrow.

All that I have written about have been known by spiritually aware individuals to a greater or lesser degrees over the passage of time. As I share some of my journey with you through my essays I hope that I will cut out all the meat and fat that surrounds the truth and allow you to get down to the bone where the truth dwells forever.

Darryl Williams

PRINCIPALS OF LIFE

I titled this section The principals of life. The reason why I chose this particular title is because I feel that every thing in this chapter were gifts. from the divine as I reached different levels of spiritual awarness. These principals became part of my life and they are what make my life calm, fulfilling and satisfied in a chaotic world. The different principals of life happen at different times and at varying degrees for everyone. The one thing that they have in common is that they all find strength in the others. My own personal spiritual journey has taught me that.

The principals of life must be continuously exercised like the body and the mind so that they can be made strong. I will be the first to tell you that this is not always easy either. The things that must be done on a day to day basis always seems to want your attention. Also unexpected situation or life's little surprises seem to always be battling for attention too. A good way to combat this is to know that all of these distractions are just the forces of evil at work trying to keep you from connecting to the true divine that is within.

I also want to tell you at this point that as you make strides in your spiritual journey there are always going to be forces at work to try and hold you back. They may come as situations, thoughts, the ego and people, yes people. I want you to be very aware that evil forces work though people. Sometimes these people even called themselves religious. They get easier and easier recognize as you grow spiritually. You may also find that you may lose or out grow some of your friends as you continue on your spiritual journey. I want you to know that the people who truly love you and are your friends will always be there no matter what. If you should lose all the people that you thought were your friends, do know that the divine will be your friend and guide you to people that are indeed true.

THE FLOW

All of the things that I write about in these essays are very personal to me. I want everyone who reads these essays in their, eternity or any part of them to know that they come from a place that is very real for me. Many of the things I share in my essays I deal with today. I am thankful that most are small and I manage them easily. Those things that are bigger take me a little while longer to get clear. It's similar to maintanence on a car, most of the time all you need to do is gas up and check the fluid levels. Sometimes however a complete tune up with an oil change is required. Spiritual maintenance is very important to me. It moves me towards a better state of spiritual existence.

I refer to this forward moving process as the flow. It took me a number of years to get on my own divine flow. When I did finally get familiar with the divine flow it took even more time for me to fully implement this flow in to all of the many aspect of my life. The primary reason why my flow took some time was do to my personality . I am the classic Type A Personality. This trait always showed up in everything that I did. Everything had to be done just right and in a specific way. Also everything in my surroundings would always have to be in perfect order all of the time. Here is what I mean. I usually spend hours cleaning each week until my house is hospital clean but if I had an event planned in a couple of days I would clean for that event too even though My house would be spotless already I have gotten a lot better however.

I also still struggle with the fact that I think that nobody can do anything for me as good as I can. There was a time when I would refuse help from some one just because I felt that I could do something more thoroughly and efficiently than the person offering to help me.

Another reason why it took some time for me to get into the divine flow was because of the intensity of how I use to structure my days. I would be making breakfast, doing laundry, washing dishes, cleaning the house and paying bills while trying to get ready for work. Crazy right! but I am sure my fellow Type A Personalities know exactly what I am talking about and you know who you are. I later discovered that it was times like these that I would be interjecting my own will instead of giving in to the divine flow.

When I was in this mode I found that I put my body, mind and spirit under an enormous amount of stress. The stress manifested itself by me feeling sick, tense, fatigued and anxious. I was poisoning myself. It all came to a peak when I had a severe anxiety attack that bordered on a nervous break down and I had to be hospitalized at the ripe old age of twenty three! Yes you heard me I said twenty three. I had no available resources left to call upon because I had used them all up by doing everything according to my flow and not giving in to the flow of the divine.

Therapy helped me to get focused and I soon saw that my attack was a blessing because I realized that I had to change my way of doing things. The thing that I had to really come to terms with was my type A personality. I had to constantly be on the look out for it so that it would not take over. I also was wise enough to know that it would be an issue that I would have to deal with for the rest of my life.

I implemented my new strategies in the way I ran my days. First I did what needed to be done and if I had time to do something afterwards I did. If I did not then it would have to wait until later, tomorrow or whenever. I must tell you that this was easier said than done. The divine flow is one of the basic realities of life. However it is a very difficult one to master. It was even harder for me because of my personality.

I struggle with giving in to the flow only sometimes now. It is something that I make a concious effort to watch out for everyday. Sometimes I fail. I am not perfect no matter what I would like to believe. I have gotten stronger as each day passes. Today when I see that I am not going with the divine flow but creating my own flow I stop and pray and surrender.

Darryl Williams

TRUTH

I had to first understand and then incorporate each principal of life into my every day existence. This integration varied in the amount of time it took depending on where I was at that time in my life. The integration had to happen in order for me to really connect with that part of me that was, is and will always be truely spiritual. The one principal that ranks first on the list of those that were hardest for me to implement was truth.

Truth was difficult for me because it meant that I had to look inside the deepest parts of my heart, mind and soul to begin to understand who I am. The truth of who I am was the hardest and very first step I had to take on my road to spirituality. It is truth that must be faced by any individual that is truly interested in a spiritual existence. Truth will always be a couragous and challenging endeavor for all and it must begin and end with self.

The truth of who I am took back to my childhood. I had to visit my childhood many times to fully understand how the things that happened to me as a child played a role in who I am today. Sometimes I uncovered things that I had locked away deep inside my heart, mind and soul for many years.

I was fortunate in that the truth of my childhood did not involve any traumatic experiences involving intentional neglect, mental, emotional, physical and sexual abuse. If this had been the case dealing with the truth could of been a long and painful experience. It may have even required professional services in order to move towards the truth.

I strongly believe that the truth of a persons past must be fully dealt with in order for that person to heal and finally move toward the truth of who they are. It will many times involve looking into the deepest parts of our hearts, minds and souls and dealing with everything that has happened to us even those things that were unpleasant. This healing is individual and personal for everyone and must happen when they are ready.

On my personal road to truth I had to go back to my childhood to deal truthfully with those things that played a role in who I am today. The biggest one was the separation of my parents. When they first separated I only got to see my dad on the weekends for about two years. He then moved to another state and I then only got to see him during the summers and Christmas. I had to truthfully acknowledge the areas in my life that not having my dad in my life constantly affected who I am.

I had went through life for many years not even realizing or admitting that my parents break up even affected me. When I was finally able to do that it then became a lesson in truth about not only me but my parents also. My parents marriage did not last because my father was a functional alcoholic. My mother endured being married to my father for ten years before she made a decision that she could not be in that marriage any longer. She was tired of the arguing and fighting that went along with my fathers drinking. It was not until I was able to be truthful with my mother about my parents marriage and about my dad before I could finally see what my mother had gone through for so many years with my father. This was hard for me because my parents kept their problems hidden from me. I was completely unaware of the turmoil that was going on at that time.

I knew that my father drank alcohol. His drinking was just another part of who he was. I never knew him any other way. I knew that my father loved me very much. He told me this often and he showed it. When I was dealing in truth I was finally able to admit to myself that my father is an alcoholic. I realized that my father had always been an alcoholic. It is also this truth that enables me to continue to love my father and accept him for who and what he is unconditionally. The only thing that I ask of him now is that when he is around me and my two boys that he is respectful of us on the few occasions that we get to see him. The truth enabled me to tell him that I expected and would not except nothing less. The truth is enpowering and is one of the realities of life that will constantly challenge me. I know that in the long run being truthful to myself will always keep me on my spiritual journey.

Living in truth will often mean dealing with things that have happened to us. Some of these things have defined who we are but the truth of these things never defines who we will become.

Darryl Williams

DIVINE ORDER

It is not by chance and it is not by my own doing that the things that have occurred in my life have happened. I know that there is a divine order that rules every aspect of my life. There are times in my life when many things are happening on any given day and not all of them are always pleasant. It is on these days that I have to remind myself that there is a divine order to all things that happening.

One of my biggest lessons in divine order happened when I had just graduated from college. I was bouncing around a few ideas in my head on what I wanted to do with myself since I had completed school. I had a feeling that I wanted to teach. The only thing about teaching was I did not really want to go into the public school system. I felt the public schools had lots of room for improvement and I wanted conditions to change before I got myself involved.

Finally after a while of weighing the pros and the cons I eventually made up my mind to go in to the public school system. I made this decision largely based on the fact that the public schools had been so kind to me, my family and my friends in the past. I figured now was as good as any time to show my gratitude. My desire was to teach the lower grades because I knew that if I was going to make a difference my chances would be greater in the lower grades of elementry school. I started to do all of the leg work involved including filling out all of the paper work need in order to get the process rolling. While I did all of this I was not feeling right about it at all.

A couple of weeks later I was vacationing in North Carolina. While there my mom, my aunt and I were talking about the day care business. My aunt had expressed an interest but her husband was not too keen on the idea because it would mean that they would have to build on to their home for the space.

On the drive back home my mom and I continued to talk about the day care business. She had a space available and I had the time so we decided to give it a shot. I knew it would take a lot to get everything together but I was excited. I knew a degree in the area would help out in the long run.

It took a few months from the time renovation began to the day the completed day care was ready. It was about another month after that before the first children started to arrive. The whole ordeal had taken a lot out of me but I felt really good about it. I know that anything worth having required a little work.

I was not totally recovered from starting my day care when I got a call from my nephew's mom. She had finally made up her mind after almost two years that my nephews would be better off with me and my mom. I was willing but I wanted the process to be done correctly, so I insisted we go through the court system. It took a lot of running around, time and court dates but in the end everything had been settled.

Divine order was definitely determining the course of my life at that time. The day care center that I had just started proved to be a huge blessing. It gave me the freedom of mobility and a flexible schedule. These two things proved to be very important because when the boys came to stay for good they needed a lot of attention. In addition to the drama that was involved in switching their schools. I had to go up to school quite often because they were having a little trouble adjusting to their new school and their new living arrangements. I was able to met them after school and help them with their homework. This was all in addition to getting therapy for them to help them cope with all that they were dealing with. It was a long and involved process for me too I must admit.

Divine order played a crucial role in my life at that time. In a short time I was able to clearly see how all of the events that were happening at that time were happening for a reason. I was being divinely groomed to deal with all of the challenges that I was going to face with being a full time dad from now on.

Today I am much better at seeing how the divine order is at work in my life now. I just have to step out of the way and let it do it's thing.

Darryl Williams

FAITH

A few years ago if anyone had asked me did I know what faith was I would of said yes and given them a definition. My definition would have been based on what I had learned from people in the church including family members. My definition would have included phrases like "You have to have faith and trust in the Lord" and "keep the faith". All would be things that I would of heard over the years. When I was done my definition of faith would be an eloquent and well-versed story. It would in fact just been a story about something that I would have had no idea of what I was talking about. I would not of been able to give a definition of faith based on my own personal experiences in life.

In the years that have pasted since I first heard all of the quotes about faith in church and in my family my life has seen its share of ups and down. I am thankful however that there has not been too many downs. The downs were important to me because these were the times that my experiences with faith were being formed.

These down times were when I experienced the true disappointments and loss that life had in store for me. It was during these disappointments and periods of loss that I was truly able to understand the true nature and power of faith. Faith started to take on a whole new meaning for me when I did not know if tomorrow would come because my heart was so heavy and I did not think I would make it through the night.

The events that have occurred in my life that began the process of me coming to understand what faith is are not really important right now. The one important thing that all of those events had in common were that they were the corner stones on which my foundation of faith were built upon. Faith began to mean even more to me as I began to quench my thirst for inner knowledge and move further along on my spiritual journey. The more I moved along on my journey the more I understood the essence of what faith truly is.

One of my most memorable experiences in faith happened when I made the decision to start my first business venture. The time that passed between me talking about opening up my first business to that actually happening was only a matter of a couple of months. During that two month period I had been putting in fifteen-hour days and doing ninety-five percent of the work that was involved in starting my first business from rehabilitation of the space that I needed to the paperwork that was involved.

The spirits blessed me during this time because I had the help of my aunt and her boss. They were very important to me and my business because both were in the business that I was about to begin. When those two months were over I was drained, tired and a little stressed.

I had not even gotten a chance to get a good nights sleep before I found myself involved in something that would totally change my life as I knew it. I was about to take on the legal responsibility for my nephews. I made the decision based totally on faith. I knew that every thing that had been happening to me in recent years was preparation for my new responsibility. I had always been a father to my nephews since they were placed on this earth. This would be different because now they would be my responsibility legally. I did not worry about what would be involved in my new responsibility at all. I had faith which meant I knew that everything was going to be alright and go according to the divine plan.

I must admit that parenthood has proven to be my most challenging and demanding job. I became a single father of two boys at one time which is a monumental task under any circumstances. The learning and reconditioning that I had to endure in order to deal with my new responsibility as a parent was possible only through my faith. It has made me see what kind of man I really am and what I am really made of. Parenthood has brought me a tremendous amount of pride and joy as well. I am thankful to the divine for showing me what faith is really all about in all aspects of my life. I know that there is still much more to come. I will be ready because now I know what I am talking about.

Darryl Williams

PRAYER

Prayer was something that I first became familiar with as a young child. My parents are both from strong southern Christian homes and that was reflected in the way that they raised my brother and me. Also my grandmothers were both highly involved in the churches that they belonged to. I spent a lot of my childhood in my grandmother's churches. It was in this environment that I began to hear most of the church rhetoric that formed a lot of my initial perception of what being a God fearing person was all about. Prayer was also a large part of the rhetoric that I was being taught in church. Prayer was a big thing in the homes of my family especially in my grandparent's homes. I had no idea of what prayer really meant. I did know that it was something that all good people who feared God did.

I recall my grandparents saying on many ocassions to "Just Pray on it" or "Pray for me" and "I will pray for you". I heard these and other things regarding prayer a lot as I was growing up. I began to practice the ritual of prayer too. I thought I understood the concept. I also wanted to be a good Christian like those that I looked up to. I only hoped that I was doing it right.

My prayers at that time typical for a child my age. I prayed for toys, money, ice cream, McDonalds, staying home from school and clothes.

As I got older my prayers became a little bit more complex. I prayed for things like good grades on test, doing well on my SAT's, passing my driving test and being excepted to those colleges that I had applied to. I became more familiar with life so the level of my prayers and the things that I prayed about became more sophisticated as time passed. However I still was not really clear on what the prayer was really about at that time.

As an adult I noticed that prayer was something that I relied on more and more as the time passed. I think it was at that particular time in my life that I began to see the true nature and power of prayer. There were many times in my life that I knew the only reason why things were happening was because I prayed for them.

It was a few years later when I began to take those first steps on my spiritual journey. It was while I was in this state of being that I began to see the true nature of prayer. Prayer was much more than a way I asked for the things I wanted in my life. As I became more and more spiritually aware and became more clear about life prayer became a part of who I was becoming. Prayer was now an important and powerful tool that I now understood. It was now what I used to open up the avenues of communication between the spirits and myself.

Prayer was now something that was completely changing life as I knew it. It was through prayer that I was able to ask for guidance when I did not have any sense of direction. Prayer was the method that I used to get many of the answers to the questions that I had about myself and about life. Those questions ranged from the most basic things like having a place to lay my head to things like finding out why I am here. Prayer has been an important instrument for me to nurture my spirit and develop the courage that I need to look inward every day in order to grow and except the things that are happening in my life.

I know that I am a vital part of the divine plan. Once I realized this I felt reborn and renewed.

The realities or principals of life are eternal and have withstood the test of time. I have come a long way on my journey and I have a ways to go still. I have been truly blessed. The spirits are now able to tell me what is around the bend and which fork in the road to take. All I have to do is just listen. I have to be honest and say that where I am at today did not happen over night and it has not been easy. Everything in life that is truly worth having is not easily gotten. Prayer has been a monumental tool in helping me to get where I am at now. It continues to help me move a long. I am truly happy to be here.

Darryl Williams

SOLITUDE/MEDITATION

There have been many evening in the past which have ended with me being totally exhausted. During the course of those days I would feel like I missed doing something important. In search of clarity I decided to look at on of my typical days for answers.

My days would be non-stop. I would be doing any and everything that needed to be done during working hours. When my work day ended I would clean up and prepare everything that was needed for the next day. Once I was home I would get dinner started and spend some time with my boys. While cooking I would be talking with the boys and trying to tie up all of the loose ends around the house. Many of these loose ends were things I would have started earlier in the day during my long lunch break. I would never finish everything most of the time though. I always seemed to have a never ending list of things to do.

Most nights I would finally just stop in the middle of what I was doing because my body would begin to just shut down. I would have to force every muscle in my body into the shower and fall in to bed afterwards. I would not eat even though I would be starving.

I would just want to sleep. I would get up eventually and eat something and go right back to sleep. The next day I would get up early in the morning before everyone else and start my whole hectic routine once again. I would be trying to get a jump start on my never ending list of things to do.

In time the spirits helped me to see why I always kept feeling like I had forgot to do something important all the time. I didn't have any solitude. I did not have a moment of total peace and quiet just for me. This stillness in the past had always been essential to me getting in touch with my spirit and meditating. I had gotten so busy doing and thinking about what I had to do from one minute to the next that I would let days even weeks pass without any solitude and meditation. The spirits showed me that all of my running around was completely pointless if I was not able to be still and quiet. This stillness was necessary in order for me to experience the divine that was giving me life to do all that I did. The solitude was also needed so I could recognize the divinity that was abundantly all around me.

It was not long before I was able to see how much I missed and needed that solitude which was crucial in order for me to hear the divine. It was this stillness that the spirits were able to give me the instructions that I needed in order for my days to run smoothly and be filled with joy. It was also during these periods of meditation that I was able to get the lessons, knowledge and wisdom that I needed so that my heart would be filled with love. This was very important because I could on any given day be the only representation of the spirit that some one may experience at all.

My life has been filled with many bends and forks in the road. I know that as long as I live I will continue to have forks and bends in the road. It is during these periods that solitude and meditation helps me to replenish my spirit and fortify my faith. I then can navigate myself along the many bends and forks in the road when they occur.

Solitude and meditation is also an important time for me because it is when I am able to receive instructions on how the spirits want me to help other people. If I am in a situation where I need to remind myself or tell someone else that there is something far greater in the universe than myself I will know what I am talking about.

Darryl Williams

PEACE

Peace is a wonderful state of being for anyone that is able to understand and implement all of the fundamentals that I write about. It is with this total understanding that they can live a truly spiritual existence. Peace however was something that completely eluded me for a time. It was not until I had been on my spiritual journey for some time that the Divine blessed me with the lesson I needed in order to find out why I did not have peace in my life.

My lesson to finding true peace took me back to the place that I often visit when I need to truely understand something. I had to go to self. This time the aspect of self took me to the very building blocks that make me who I am. I am talking about my genetic makeup. This would be where I would uncover the traits that kept true peace out of my grasp.

My task would prove to be difficult because I had to look at myself honestly and with untainted eyes. I was able to do it and I had to go to the area of my genetic makeup where my problem was. It was my personality traits. The ones that kept peace just out of my reach were that I am a chronic worrier and perfectionist. I also have an intense and strong drive. These combinations of traits were toxic for me on more than just a few occasions.

My next step on my quest for peace was to find out two important things. The when and why of these aspects of my personality began. I had to go back to my childhood for the answers that I needed.

31

It all started when I was eight years old my parents went their separate ways. A direct result of my parent's separation was that my mom began to work more hours. She did this largely because she wanted to make sure that my brother and I had the things that we needed and some of the things that we wanted too. While my mom worked I took on the responsibilities of running the house. My brother was older than I was but he was not as mentally and emotionally mature as I was. His shortcomings at that time left me in charge.

I did everything I cooked, cleaned and went to the grocery store. I also had the worrying that came along with the very adult responsibilities I had a such at young age. I became the caretaker of my family. I wanted everything that I did to be just right so that my mother would be pleased. I knew that she worked hard to provide for my brother and me and I did not want her to have to do too much after working long hours all day.

I discovered that it was during this time in my life that the groundwork was being laid that would eventually lead me to becoming a perfectionist, chronic worrier and having a strong drive. Half of my journey into my childhood was complete. I now knew when my genetically motivated personality traits began. The next thing I needed to know was why.

My mother is both a perfectionist and a chronic worrier also but it is a little different. Her worrying was centered on making sure her family had so in turn she worked harder and harder to provide. Her perfectionism manifested itself in her work and on her job where she spent most of her time naturally. I spent my pre- teens, teens and young adulthood taking care of my family with such zest that I could stand up to the best of them. My father had given me his strong drive and working hard at a task until it was completed. In taking care of my family once I started on something I did not stop until every detail was completed and I worked very hard at doing that.

The second half of my journey into my childhood was complete. I understood when and why my personality began to take hold. My parents had given me quite a legacy of genes to content with.

As I got older my genetically motivated personality traits got even worst. I did everything myself because I always felt like no one could do anything for me as good as I could. I became a grab the bull by the horns kind of person. When something had to be done I just did it.

When I was well into my adulthood my genetically fueled personality traits always had me on the go and in fast forward mode. I felt like I was going to run out of time before I did all the things that I needed to be done. It did not matter if I got up very early in the morning to start my day I always felt as if I was behind. I had done more by eight o'clock than most people would have done all day. Most morning I always found myself with ten minutes in the morning to shower and get myself ready for work before eight. I was now at a point in my life where I was really messed up. My uncontrolled personality traits had robbed me of all peace in my life and I was really paying a high price. I was physically, mentally, emotionally and spiritually sick. I had to make a change my very existence depended on it.

It was at this point in my life when I prayed heavily for the spirits to guide me towards peace. All of my personality traits led me to believe that I was in total control of my life and I was not. I now understood why I was the way I was and I now wanted to move on to the road that would lead me to peace. My prayers were answered and I surrendered to the spirits and begun the process of living in a peaceful manner. This meant that I had to re-learn a new way of living and thinking. I had to apply my new way of living and thinking to all aspects of my life.

It has proven to be a formidable challenge and I have failed many times. I have had to go against my very nature many times in order to have peace. This is not always easy. I use to battle with it everyday. Today I am much better. It will always be something I will have to be concious of. It's in my genes after all.

JOY

There was a time not to long ago when my life for a time primarily consisted of taking care of my two sons, running a small business, cleaning, cooking and washing clothes. There are many duties or task that I could add to the list of things that I did. If I did then I would have a list that would be as long as Santa Clause's wish list. Let's just say that I was a pretty busy bee. I was constantly on the go doing this and doing that. I had an all day job that from the time that I got up until the time that I went to bed consisted of me taking care of people. My only relief was at night when I got the nights off in order to sleep most of the time.

In case you haven't figured it out by now. I was suffering from a major case of 'Super Man Syndrome'. I was Super-dad, Super-uncle, Super-son, Super-nephew, Super-Cousin, Super-Grandson, Super-Mr. Fix It and Super Mr. problem solver.

All of the titles that I had gave me a since of worth. I felt needed, depended on, and valued but I was not fulfilled. I felt so empty inside and I was also very unhappy. I began to do even more in an attempt to try and not think about how empty and unhappy I was. In the end that tactic proved not to work at all. I was not only feeling empty, unfulfilled and unhappy now I could add exhausted to the list..

My emotional unrest was happening at a time in my life when I felt that I was on my spiritual journey. I did not completely understand why I was feeling the way I did. The spirits helped me to become clear and see what my true problem was. I had no time for me. I was so busy making

35

decisions all of the time for everyone else at the drop of a dime. I had completely over looked me. Each time that I overlooked me I missed out on my chance to get still and pray. My spirits helped me to understand that I had not been using the most powerful tool that I had. It was my power to be still and pray.

Shortly afterwards I got still and prayed for guidance. I had prayed countless times before but this time was definitely different. I knew that my very sanity was at stake. I asked the spirits to guide me and give me the answers to the questions had. In time the spirits helped me to see that I had no joy in my life! I was not doing anything just for me that brought me joy! I let the Super Man Syndrome along with dealing with life's daily drama put myself further and further down the list of things that were important. This process did not happen over night but when it was complete I was joyless. I had even stopped writing. The one constant thing in my life that had always brought me joy all the time.

I said to myself at that moment that I was going to do the things that make me happy and bring me my joy right now! My own joy was now my number one priority. I made up my mind that every day from now on everybody else would have to either wait or be put on hold for a while so that I could do the things that brought me joy. Writing was the number one thing on the list.

It was that very same day that I realized that God gives us all certain talents. We must use these talents to honor God and show that we are thankful for our blessings. I was not only not honoring myself I was not honoring God. I had just been blessed with an idea for a new writing project. The project would be two fold for me. First, It would give me the oppurtunity to potentially help many people. Secondly It would allow me in a very small way to thank God and the Spirits for their countless blessings to me over the years.

When I made the decision to begin writing again, I realized that my spirit had been struggling to free itself from my self induced prison for a long time. I had finally set it free and that brought me an enormous amount of joy that I had not experienced in quite sometime. I now realize that one of the most important things I can do for myself is to do the things in my life that bring me joy. It may even mean that people will have to wait even the ones that I love and hold dear.

Darryl Williams

WISDOM

I have come a long way since I began my spiritual journey into self-exploration and the truths of Life. I can still remember where I used to be and how far the spirits have brought me so far. I have truly been blessed and I am thankful. While I have been on my spiritual journey the spirits have given me the oppurtunity to experience many mystical and magical things. One of the magical gifts that I had been given was wisdom. I was given the gift of wisdom a long time ago. However, It was not until I was able to progress in my spirituality and become clear that I saw how important the blessing of wisdom has been in my life.

Wisdom is one of my blessings that the more and more I used it the better it becomes. I can not recall the exact day and time that I began using my blessing. I can recall little incidents that happened years ago where wisdom was the only thing that kept me from making the wrong decision.

One such incident was when my brother and his friends would stay home from school. I joined them a couple of times too, but it was wisdom that made me realize that I needed to be in school. One other such incident was when an older boy that I knew came to my door to tell me that I had gotten a bad letter from school and it had been accidentally put into his mailbox. He refused to give me the letter unless I let him in to my apartment. I was really scared because I did not want my mother to find out about the letter so I thought about letting him in. It was the blessing of wisdom that told me not to. I don't know what would have happened to me if I had let him in and I am glad that wisdom kept me from finding out.

When I became a teenager it was wisdom that allowed me to resist the temptation of drugs, alcohol, and sex and graduate from high school. While I was in college I went through my experimental phase that included drugs, alcohol and sex and peer pressure. The blessing of wisdom helped me to see that those things were not doing me any good and were not getting me anywhere so I stopped them soon after I began. It was wisdom and the spirits blessing me with a wonderful mother that allowed me to stay in college and graduate. I am currently raising two boys as a single parent and I must admit that it is quite a challenge. It has been through wisdom that I know that I am not doing it alone. I don't want any one to believe that I have not made some wrong choices in my life because I have. In those situations it has been wisdom that has allowed me to see my mistakes and change them. Wisdom can come at different times and in many forms. I know that however it comes and however hard it may be I am ready.

PATIENCE

I have had to learn many things since being placed on this earth. I like to call the things that I have learned so far my lessons. It took me many lessons and time before I realized that one of the primary reasons why I was put on this earth was to learn.

Sometimes the lessons that I had to learn were not always pleasant. In fact my most important lessons usually came along with some pain. It has only been after I became clear that I am able to see how in the past I use to get so caught up in the circumstances that surrounded a particular lesson that I would never get it. I would have to repeat the same lesson or something similar until I would learn what I needed to learn.

Today I am better at focusing on the lesson and not the who, when, why and how of it. I also know that many of my important lessons in life had to be modified sometimes as well. As I grew, expanded, and my experiences changed my life lessons have to grow and expand also. The life lesson that I find that I constantly have to modify often is patience.

One of my earliest lessons with patience happened when I was a young child and my parents decided to go their separate ways. I had always had both of my parents around me and when they went their separate ways I had to learn certain things. Patience was one of those things that I had to learn in order to help me cope with only being able to see my dad on the weekends.

41

A couple of years had passed and I had gotten use too seeing my dad on the weekends. He then suddenly moved to another state. It was at that time that I had to relearn patience in a new way so that I was able to deal with only being able to see my dad now only twice a year. Those times were during the summer and at Christmas time.

I was in my late teens when my next memorable lesson in patience happened. It was not as direct as my prior lessons but it was just as powerful. My mom and I had finally sat down and talked about the reasons and that her and my dad went their separate ways. I think at that time I was fully able to understand on a level that I would not of before.

Prior to my conversation with my mom I remembered my father drinking, but the thing that stood out in my head was that he being gentle and loving to my brother and I. I heard everything that my mother told me about my dad but I don't think that I fully understood what my mother had gone through. I just was patient again and I knew that I would understand when it was time.

I was much older when I started observing my father with an intensity that I had never done before. I can still recall him being so drunk that he would make a spectacle of himself often. I could see how he became a totally different creature when he was under the influence of alcohol. He would irritate me in such a way that I would be very angry with him and also embarrassed.

The list that I kept silently in my head began to add up as time passed. Then a few years ago I got a call from my father's brother that lived in the same town as my dad. He had told me that my father was very ill and had pneumonia. I was of course very concerned and wanted to know what happened. I was told that my father was found in a ditch in freezing weather. He had passed out and fallen there because he was so drunk. When he recovered my dad went back to doing the same amount of drinking that he had been doing. It was then that I finally fully understood what my mom and I had talked about so many years earlier.

It was a turning point in my life because I had finally accepted who and what my dad was. Patience was instrumental in me being able to become totally clear. I know that I have been blessed and I strive for a deeper understanding of all situations with each passing day. Many of my life's lessons have had to be relearned. It's been a positive experience for me because change and growth has taken place. I am an earthly representation of my creator. I could not be that in a stagnate environment.

Darryl Williams

ACCEPTANCE

Acceptance is a principle that I thought I had accepted and implemented into my life. I had accepted many situations in my life. The two that were the most difficult for me to accept involved my family. I had accepted the fact that I had a father that struggles with alcohol dependency and a sibling that struggles with alcohol and chemical dependency along with all the other issues that come along with addiction. Once I accepted these things accepting everything else that life had in store for me seemed to not be a little easier.

As the time passed and I continued to make strides in my spirituality acceptance was one of the principal that I thought I was becoming more comfortable with. I just learned recently that I was not applying the rules of acceptance equally to everybody. I was putting my friends and the people whom I love in a different category. I have always been the type of person that has high expectations from the people that are close to me and whom I love. Many of my friends and some family members fall into this category. I had been unknowingly letting my high expectations of these people in my life get in the way of me fully accepting them. The incident that helped me to fully understand what I had been doing for years involved a close friend of mine. I have been a friend with this person for the past ten years. In the ten years that we have been friends we have seen, heard, talked and expierenced a lot of things together. In the time that we have been friends my friend has done many things that I felt were silly, dumb or just plain stupid. Most of these things have been issues surrounding relationships, family, employment and people that he knew. When these bad experiences were over I always thought that he would learn and apply these lessons to his life. My expectations were always high and I was dissapointed because he never seemed to apply any lessons he had learned.

I had not been communicating with him over the past three months because I was annoyed with him because of some things that he had done that I did not understand. I had been trying to help him get his life together because according to him he wanted more. My friend had very little motivation and was not even trying to meet me half way so I stopped. This was not the first time that he had done this but my expectations were high. I was dissapointed. My friend had begun a new relationship immediately after ending one just a couple of weeks before. I knew that my friend was needy and needed some one around all the time. This was not the first time that this had happened but my expectations were high and I was dissapointed. My friend had not paid their phone bill so the out going service was off. I had called one day shortly after and the number was totally disconnected. I was upset because I knew that my friend had some one living with them. I felt my friend could do badly alone. I was dissapointed again. I had not spoken to my friend for a few weeks and I knew it was due to the new relationship they were in. This had happened before yet I still had high expectations. I was disappointed again. This time the disappointment turned into anger. I let the anger keep me from speaking to my friend.

I stayed angry until I begun to see where the root of my anger was coming from. The spirits helped me to realize that I had to stop automatically having high expectations from my friends and my loved ones. It did not matter how

46

much I love a person or how good of a friend I considered them to be. These people are human and are capable of making some mistakes. Unfortunately these mistakes are repeated over and over again. The spirits helped me to see that I should not be angry with my friend. Over the years that I had known my friend they had demonstrated to me that I should not have had such high expectations for them in the first place. I should just allow my friend to be who they always were and love them unconditionally.

Once I got clear with that the spirits helped to accept the fact that just because I was making strides in my spirituality did not mean that my friends were. Every one has to look for his or her own happiness and I could not wish anything for anyone. I know how good it is but every one has to come when they are truly ready.

Acceptance is a concept that I try to put in to every aspect of my life now. I have seen that by doing this It has uncomplicated my life tremendously. It greatest impact has been in helping me to perfect the avenues of communication that I have with the spirits. I find that the spirits are communicating with me on a constant basis now as I go through my days. There are days when they have a lot to say to me. It can ranges from simple things like ordering my days so that they run smoothly to completing task that help me to achieve the goals that the spirits have allowed me to set for myself. I know that I must be in a concious state of acceptance in order to be able to take in all that the spirits have for me. This sometimes include acting on the directions of the spirits without question.

Darryl Williams

HUMOR

I have always had a good sense of humor. I recall being a big prankster in school. I used to get into a lot of trouble because of it. It wasn't so bad because as soon as the heat would blow over I was looking for my next big laugh. I remained that way until I got into high school. Naturally I was a little older and my sense of humor became a little more sophisticated. I must admit that it's those early gut busting, tear jerking laughs that leave you gasping for air that make up my funniest memories. The humor that I developed at that time is the essence of my humor today.

A couple of years ago I began to notice that I was not having any of those gut-busting laughs any more. I would be out with my friends and they could be talking about the funniest thing or making fun of some one and all I would do is just chuckle. I found that I really would be holding back laughter esspecially if some one were being made fun of. I was becoming a stick in the mud. I was the first one to say "stop laughing" or "that's not funny" to the people I was with. I would want to laugh but for some reason I just could not. I had gotten to the point where I had just stopped laughing. I had become very serious and that was so unlike me. I had lost my humor, which up until then was a big part of who I was. I knew something was wrong.

I thought about the reason for the change and after some soul searching. I eventually traced my problem to my newly found spiritual development. I discovered that as I moved further along on my spiritual journey I laughed a lot less and became very serious. Some how I felt that if I was cracking jokes, laughing at people or just being my normal

49

silly self my newly developed spirituality would some how seem less valid. I had done a really good job of convincing myself that I had to stifle my naturally humorous nature and control any outward display of it. I thought that if I did not then I was not being a true representative of the spirits.

I am happy to say that it was not long after my realization that the spirits helped me to see how very wrong I was. The spirits allowed me to get clear and understand that humor is just one of the many gifts that they have blessed me with. It is my humor that makes me a unique human. In time I began to shed all of the fear and guilt that I had put on due to my lack of understanding. I know now from where my humor comes. In no time I was laughing at myself, with my love ones and all the people that I encountered. I began to see how funny we as humans can be and make light of that fact. My experience with regaining my humor helped me to realize how alike we all are and how much we share co existing on this planet.

Regaining my humor taught me something else also. I see how laughter releases my body of the daily stresses that I encounter in my everyday exsistence. When I am laughing I am able to forget about all of the little things that are running around in my head and just be me. Often it is in this state of just being me that I can connect to the Spirits and be true to myself. I can not express to you how wonderful it is to be true to myself and know that the spirits are with me always. This happens when I am laughing or when I am crying. Humor is a marvelous gift that we all have been given as offspring of the Divine. We must use it to show our gattitude.

COURAGE

We all have things in our lives that we have dreamed about doing or things that we have not quite got around to doing. Let's call them hopes and dreams. These hopes and dreams can be something monumental like quitting a dead end job that you only took because the benefits were good and opening that business that you always wanted. These hopes and dreams can also be something little like calling in sick and spending the day bumming around at the beach reading romance novels.

I have such hopes and dreams. Some of which are things that I have wanted to do since I was a child. Some are things that have passed in my head just last night.

I have been fortunate because since I began my spiritual journey I have done a lot of the things that I have hoped and dreamed about. I must admit that I have not yet done them all because there are still many more I have to do. I was able to do these things because of courage. It has meant the my difference between me being an active participant in hopes and dreams or sitting on the sidelines wishing.

The courage that I am speaking about is a courage that I was only able to receive after I became spiritually aware. Since I started the process of looking inwards for the answers to I had. I have been blessed with an assortment of very powerful tools that I utilize every day of my life. Courage is one of my tools when used correctly make a difference in my own quality of life. My courage is not some thing that was not given to me just over night just because I desired it. It has come through years of self-exploration and facing the reality of who and where I am. Also why I do the things that I do or not do. The courage I have is another spiritual muscle that I have been given. The more I use it the bigger it becomes.

I want you to understand that just because I have the blessing of courage it does not work alone. There are other tools that work with it. I have the courage to put my hand in a pot of boiling water but don't. I also have the courage to take every dime that I have and go out and spend it on an extravagant house or car but I don't. I also have the blessing of wisdom. It is another tool that works along with courage. I have courage and the wisdom to know when and what to be courageous about.

GRATITUDE

Gratitude is a very important principal. It functions as a one of the spiritual catalyst. Gratitude works like a doorman holding the doors to our souls open so that the Spirit of the divine can enter freely. Gratitude creates a guest room in our life so that the Spirit always has a place to stay.

My heart felt gratitude allows the spirit to enter my soul freely and have a place to stay always. This spiritual bond has given me many blessings. The combination of these blessings has allowed me to have clarity. Clarity has made me absolutely sure that anything is possible. It has been my clarity that has allowed my roots to go deep into the soil and kept me standing when the storms of confusion and chaos come blowing strong.

One Christmas I got a chance to tell someone that I love the importance of gratitude. Christmas has always been a special time for me because it is the one time of year that I get a chance to see me dad, grandparents and other family members that I don't otherwise get to see during the year. In addition to that this particular Christmas turned out to be really memorable because I was able to tell some one I loved the importance of gratitude.

Christmas had ran along smoothly with out any major catastrophes. I did not let anyone in my family get to me at all not even my dad. The day before I was to leave to come back home I got a phone call from a relative that I had not gotten a chance to see yet. She told me that she needed to talk to me and without hesitation I agreed. I knew that she had some taxing things that were going on in her life recently. One of which has been taking care of a sick parent whom had developed multiple problems which required round the clock care. She was also dealing with her own medical problem that was giving her an enormous amount of discomfort and pain. I was also told by other family members that she had recently broken up with her fiancée after finding out that he had not only been unfaithful but had married someone else.

During my conversation with her she told me a lot of things. Some of the things I knew about and others I did not. She expressed to me that she had contemplated suicide on several occasions. I looked into her eyes as she told me her story and I saw so much pain and despair in her eyes. I reassured her and told her that I understood because I too had felt so overwhelmed that suicide seemed like an option. I began to tell her some things that had happened in my life and how I was able to gain control over all of those things in time through prayer and help from the divine. It was in that very instance that I realized something very important. I am a representative of the divine and my words are the voice in which the divine can speak. It was one of many periods of enlightenment that I have experienced.

I assured her that things were going to be fine. I let her know that some times things happen to us for very specific reasons. I could see that she was really caught up in the circumstances that were going on in her life and that she was not able to recognize her blessings. I let her know that life will get difficult at times. It is during these times that the spirit gives us the tools we need in order to get over, around or under obstacles in order to move forward. I told her that being able to show gratitude to the spirits is a very important thing even in times when we don't feel like we have a lot to be thankful for. It is the simple act of saying thank you that allows the divine spirit to enter into our soul and have a place to flourish in us all.

I told her that my gratitude is a very humbling thing for me. It allows me to acknowledge that there is a force that is more powerful than I am. It is this force that is responsible for my very exsistance. When I am thankful it allows me to be receptive to all of the things that the Spirits has to offer me. Sometimes I am not able to see these things right away. Often there are a series of steps that I must go through in order to achieve my ultimate blessing. I do know that showing gratitude for even the smallest of things that I have makes a difference for me. It can make a seemingly bad day a great one and I have a reason to smile. I let her know that whatever she needs to do next lay in her hands.

Darryl Williams

INTEGRITY

I thought that I was finished with all of the essays that were going to go into this collection. I then kept adding this or changing that for the sake of clarity. While in the mist of my editing craze the word integrity kept popping into my head which made me even more crazy.

Later I saw the lesson the spirit was trying to show me. The spirit was letting me know that as long as I am a representative of the Divine then my work will never be done. There will always be something to add or something that needs clarifying. The next essay is real example of that fact.

Integrity is just one of the many arsenal that the spirit has given me to navigate my way along my journey. Integrity has allowed me to stand my ground and make some tough decisions when it really mattered. One of those occasions that stands out in me mind, where my integrity came into play happened to me a few years ago.

I was dating someone whom I later found out was married. I was told that they were separated. It was mutually agreed that they both would move on with their lives and this had been the case for a few years now. There were children from the marriage so I knew that there would always be a relationship because they shared children. I was also told that they still were very good friends though. I felt dating this person should not be a problem because everything seem to have been on the table. I also knew that people have a way of telling you what they think you want to hear in order to get what they want.

Many months passed and over the course of those months the person that I had cautiously decided to date showed me they were serious about getting to know me. There were many things that were said and more importantly done that made me let down my guard. Naturally I started to care for this person. I was having a great time and everything was going great.

One evening I was told that the spouse whom they were separated from was coming to visit family and friends. I knew there was a very real chance that the person that I was dating would be paid a visit too. This did not bother me because I knew that they were still friends in addition to the fact that they shared children. There was also a part of me that was uncomfortable too. I knew that a divorce had not been finalized yet either. I wanted to know more in order to make me feel more at ease.

The best way to find out information is to ask questions and that is what I did. The questions were a series of what ifs? I asked questions like what if the "ex" decided to visit where would they stay? What if they wanted to stay with you would you let them? What if the "ex" did stay where would they sleep? What if the "ex" wanted to sleep in your bed with you? What if your "ex" wanted to do more with you than sleep? I knew that I was asking tough questions but I was not feeling right about this whole situation at all.

My discomfort was a direct message from the spirit. It was because of these series of questions that I found out that the "ex" had no idea that I was more than just a friend. I thought that odd being that they were such good friends and that we had been dating for nearly a year.

I was not at all satisfied with the answers that I got. I also was terribly bothered by the fact that I was portrayed as just a casual friend. I then had to evaluate everything that had taken place in my life in the past year. Everything that I was told and shown in the past year were doubtful to me now. I ultimately made the decision that I could not continue seeing this person.

My integrity would not allow me to be true to myself and the values that were important to me. I could not continue with the relationship any further. I had developed feelings for the person I was dating and my decision was tough and caused me some pain. It took me many months to heal and to move on. I was very thankful though because the spirit had blessed me with integrity. It was that integrity that kept me from having to deal with a situation that could of been a whole lot worse had I decided to continue a relationship with that person. When all was said and done I still had something very important my integrity.

Darryl Williams

NON- JUDGMENT

The principle of non-judgment is one that was easy for me to understand. I knew I understood it when I was able to look at an individual and know that the things that are going on in that persons life has everything to do with them. Their situation in life has everything to do with the decisions and choices that they have made for themselves. It has everything to do with the lessons about life that they must learn. Implementing the principal into my everyday life was where the difficulty laid.

My real challenge in being non judgmental comes when it involves people that I love. The love that I have for my friends and certain family members has made it hard for me not to be judgmental all the time. There has been times when I have failed and made a judgment on someone that I love.

It has been my blessing of clarity that has helped me with implementing non- judgment into my life even with the people that I love the most. Now I can look at my love ones and be okay with the who, what, why, and where they are in their lives.

I don't want to give the impression that practicing non-judgment is an easy thing. It is not easy an easy principal at all. When I think that I have it mastered something always comes up to challenge me. It is during these times that I must pray so that I can remain clear.

Non Judgment is something that I can practice today with relative ease and most days it does not require any special effort from me at all. I am sure that I will still have many instances where it will be difficult. When this happens I will have to ask the spirit for the strengh I know that can only be provided by the divine.

FORGIVENESS

Forgive and forget is a phase that I first remember hearing as a small child. My mother was in fact the one person in my life who I heard say it the most. I would hear her saying forgive and forget often during her many conversations with her friends and family especially my aunts whom she is close to. I also heard it said to people she just casually knew. I had absolutely no idea at that time what forgive and forget meant. The only thing I did know was that my mother always said those words during conversation with someone that was upset about something somebody had done.

I was able to figure out to the best of my abilities at a young age what forgive and forget meant. It did not seem like anything to difficult to do. If my mother said it all the time then it must be good. I was a child and children are experts at forgiving and forgetting. In fact during that time I can remember many instances when I would have had the biggest fight with a friend or my brother and the hours later we would be laughing and playing together as if nothing ever happened.

As I got older the whole notion of forgive and forget was still something that was not difficult for me to do. It was not until I started to enter into my adult years that I started to feel that there was something fundamentally wrong with the whole idea of forgiving and forgetting. During those early years of adulthood I have been upset with quite a few individuals who had did or said things to hurt me. I an eventually would calm down and in time I would be able to forgive them. It was the forgetting part that I was having trouble with.

It was not until years later when I was making strides in my spiritual development that I began making the connection that I needed to make. My spiritual development allowed me to see why the forgetting part of the phrase forgive and forget was such a difficult thing for me to do.

It all goes back to one of the most important and basic lessons that I have ever learned since I have had spiritual clarity in my life. It is the knowledge that I was put on this earth to experience the lessons in life that the spirits have to offer me. The culmination of these lessons for me so far has been many blessing that I will carry with me forever.

All of these blessing have been valuable to me and have helped make me into the spiritual being that I am today. Most of my lessons have been good experiences but some have been painful People have been a big part of many of my lessons the good and the painful ones too. I was able to forgive these people because I ultimately knew they were important instruments to me receiving a lesson. My understanding of a lesson eventually leads me to a blessing.

I have not had anything that has happened to me that I would ever want to forget. This includes all of my life lessons and the people that played a role in my lessons even if they were not pleasant. If I forget about any part of my lesson than my whole learning experience along with it's blessing would have been in vain. I would ultimately at some point or another have to repeat these experiences again. I quite honestly would rather spend my time enjoying the blessings that I have already aquired than repeating them because I forgot.

Forgiving and forgetting is not something that I recommend that anyone should do. I believe in foregiving whole heartedly but forgetting just wastes precious time, energy and spirit.

Darryl Williams

COMPASSION

I would like to present the following situation to you in order for you to think about what your response would be if you were in the same situation. One day after you had spent most of the day at the mall catching all the sales and you were reaching for the door to exit the mall when you hear a cry in the distance. When you turn to see where the cry is coming from a child runs up to you visible shaken and in tears and says "I am lost". What would you do? The answer to this question would depend on a very real emotion called compassion that we all have in greater or lesser degrees.

I consider myself to be a very compassionate person. In recent years as I have grown spiritually I have had to have various lessons on compassion. The spirits have allowed me to realize the importance of compassion in my life. Compassion is a very precious resource that I have and I have to be very careful about how I distribute this valuable commodity.

I have learned that just because a person is a family member, friend or someone that I am familiar with does not mean that these individuals should automatically get compassion from me. When I think about it out of all the people that I have had to deal with it has been the people that I care for the most that have least deserved my compassion.

They have been living their lives the way they wanted to. Many of them have done things in their lives and made decisions that have been wrong constantly. They have let the lessons that the divine has offered to them be in vain and continue to repeat the same mistakes year after year and not honor the Divine.

In all fairness I know that we are all entitled to our share of mistakes and growing pains. I am not referring to those things. I am talking about the concious choices a person makes to deal with people and situations they know are not good for them repeatedly. In situations like these if a person does not choose to learn a lesson and move ahead then it is no longer a mistake it is a choice.

I know many people that fit into the category I have just described. Some of these people at one time have been my closest friends and dearest family members. Compassion however is something that I can no longer give these people. The Spirit has shown me that my resource of compassion should only be used on people and in situations that deserve it. I have learned that if I use it on people and situations that are not deserving then it gets used up very quickly.

This is dangerous because there may be a person or situation that may come in to my life who really deserves my compassion and I do not want to be all out because I did not manage my precious resource well. I am at a point in my life were I am not willing to take any chances of depleting my reserve of compassion or any of my other resources for that matter. I know that there are still many situations and people that will come into my life that will need them. I want my reserves to be full and intact.

In the beginning of this essay I presented a situation to you and then asked what would you do? I would like to believe that your reaction would not be any different than any other compassionate human being faced with a similar situation.

Darryl Williams

IN MEMORY OF

While working on this book I had to deal with the death of my grandmother. My grandmother had been a strong force in my life. During my childhood she was a positive role model and instilled a lot in me. As an adult my grand mother became my friend as well as a powerful spiritual resource for me as well. She was very familiar with the power of that which is divine, which was another unique connection we had.

Her death was particularly devastating to me because I had never had anyone close to me die. I had to endure grief and pain in a way I had never known. It was my first time ever mourning someone death and it affected me in a huge way. The grief and pain left me horribly depressed. The depression affected everything that was going on in my life at that time. I lost my motivation to do many things including writing. I just did not want to deal with anything or anyone at any time at all.

I felt many things while I was dealing with all of my grief. The two that I remember most were a loss of control and guilt. I felt there was nothing I could do to save my grandmother and I felt guilty about not being able to make everything all right. In time I started to heal and was able to move on. It took some time but it was something that I know I would have to do for myself.

Since my grandmothers death she has spoken to me many times and has helped me deal with my feelings of guilt and lose of control. Missing her can be difficult at times. Knowing she is still a spiritual force in my life has empowered me and given me freedom. My last essay is called Freedom. I wrote it with her in mind, body and spirit.

FREEDOM

Freedom is something that I thought that I had. I knew I could go any place I wanted to go and express what was on my mind without fear. I knew I was able to shop in any store that I want to and eat in any restaurant that I desired. I could choose who I wanted to represent me from my local community leader to the president. All of those things are important examples of what freedom is in the context of the society in which I am a part. Yet, I still was not as free as I thought. My true freedom was not something that I was completely aware of.

The type of freedom that I came to know is a different kind of freedom. It is more personal and lasting than any other type of freedom that I can think of. It is the freedom that became available to me once I accepted the spirits as an intrical part of my life. It is a freedom that is grounded in truth and is thriving and constantly growing.

I have to be honest and tell you that my journey to spiritual freedom has not been an easy one. Over the years there were many lessons that I had to learn and some were difficult to say the least. The freedom that I have been blessed with however has been worth any difficulties that I had to endure along the way. The freedom that I have aquired on my spiritual journey is always evolving and is only bond by my own human limitations. These limitations are always present both actual or perceived. Here is a brief episode in my life in which my human limitations were robbing me of my full freedom potential.

I was running my own day care business, which any one who has any experience with children knows this requires a lot out of a person. I had the monumental responsibility of raising two preteen boys on my own. My family helped out a lot especially my mom but most of the load fell on me. I was dealing with the stresses of running my household and my mom also because she was always working or traveling; in addition to dealing with all of the stress that come along with everyday life.

While all of this was going on in my life I took on the additional task of starting this book. It's not hard to see that my plate was more than full. One of my very real human limitations is that I am a chronic over achiever. It was this mindset that lead me to belief that I could pull off all that I was doing with out a hitch. Guess what? It did not work.

I had once again put my emotional well being, mind, body and spirit in a compromising predicament. I felt like I was losing my mind I did not have anytime for myself to pray, meditate, rest, or just have good old fun. I was on a downward spiral and at the heart of it all. I was losing all of the precious freedom that I had gained on my spiritual journey. My spirits came to my rescue to tell me the things I needed to change in order to clean up the mess that I had made and move ahead to my next level of freedom.

In a short time the spirits gave me the instructions I needed that lead up to me only having to run my business for three to four hours a day. I also had a couple of financial blessing that for divine reasons happened in the midst of my restructuring period. I put the kids and myself on a budget and it worked. My freedom this time came in the form of having my days free so I cold work on my book more comfortably or any other thing that I like doing.

My spiritual freedom is an important part of the spiritual journey that I am on. This freedom is also intricately wrapped up in all aspects of my life and all the things that I do or not do. True freedom is a wonderful thing for me. It is a very real manifestation of the power of my own spiritual accomplishments and all of the divine entities that have allowed me to be where I am. I wish you all FREEDOM.

Darryl Williams

REFLECTION

I have outlined a number of principals of life I feel are important in spiritual development. These principals have proven to be essential tools for me when I began my spiritual journey. Today they continue to be enhanced and enriched as I grow but the core of what they are is unchanging and timeless.

My purpose in writing about these things are to in some form or another arouse somebody's spirit. Once that spirit is aroused I wanted the realities and principals and concepts to be on the mind of the spiritually aroused. I want them to be thought about, rethought and thought about again until they are understood in a way that is comfortable to whom ever is seeking understanding.

There are not any time limits and there are no right or wrong ways any one has to adhere to in regard to trying to get clear about any of the principals that I have spoken about. It must be done in a way that is right and in the time frame of the interpreter. This process may take some time in happening. It has a lot to do with what a person has been through, is going through and will go through in their life. It may take many months or even years

Also there is not a certain order to the principals of life. They were not laid out in any particular way in the book because I felt that one was more important than the other was. They are all equal in terms of their power and their impact. You could start with the very last one and read backwards it does not matter. The affect will still be the same. I can say that they have all positively impacted my life in ways that are too numerous to mentioned. The key to the realities of life and the principals that I have mentioned are that they need to be lived. They need time to be challenged, questioned, expanded and reinforced.

INSPIRATIONS

The Spirit has been very gracious by allowing me to experience many moments of wisdom over the years. In many instances this wisdom has come to me in the form of words. These words of wisdom were important reminders of my countless blessings and the power that has been given to me by the spirits. I have had these words of wisdom hanging up in up my house in various places for years. Their purpose serves to humble me and remind me of who is responsible for all that I have. I get a chance to share them with all who visit my home. I want to share these words with you in hopes that they will at the very least remind you of how much you have to be thankful for.

Darryl Williams

<u>ETERNAL WISDOM</u>

1. DAILY RECOGNITION & GRATITUDE.
2. ASK AND YOU SHALL HAVE.
3. ALL NEEDS ARE FULFILLED, ALLOWING TOTAL DEDICATION TO THE MISSION.
4. SELF HAS TO BE OVER LOOKED FOR A HIGHER GOOD.
5. ALLOW NO PERSON, PLACE OR THING TO KEEP YOU FROM THE MYSTICAL, MAGIC TOTALNESS OF THE POWER.
6. SATAN (EVIL) IS ALWAYS ACTIVE. HE CAN TAKE MANY FORMS AND IS PRETTILY PACKAGED RECOGNIZE HIS EXSISTENCE.
7. IF NOT OF THE SPIRITS, BY THE SPIRITS THEN IT COULD NEVER BE YOURS.

Darryl Williams

GOLDEN RULES FOR NOW

- **Daily Healing Time**
  (Spirit, Mind, Body, Soul)

- **Body Is A Gift, Treat It
  As Such.**

- **Haste, Tension& Stress
  Rob Us Of Our Joy.**

- **NoOne Is Perfect, Allow
  People To Be ThemSelves.**

Darryl Williams

THINGS TO REMEMBER

I MUST PAY ATTENTION TO MY INNER VOICE.
IT SPEAKS FOR A REASON.
I AM NOT ABLE TO HELP EVERY ONE.
I WILL TRY NOT TO PROCRASTINATE.
I WILL NOT BE AFRAID OF THE UNKNOWN.
I WILL NOT BE AFRAID OF SUCCESS.
2 TIMOTHY VERSE 7
-FOR GOD HAS NOT GIVEN US A SPIRIT OF
FEAR, BUT OF POWER AND OF LOVE AND A
SOUND MIND.
I WILL TRY AND ACKNOWLEDGE THAT I AM:
-PEACE
-KNOWLEDGE
-FREEDOM
-CHOICE
I AM MOST THANKFUL FOR MY
FRIENDMILY = FRIENDS/FAMILY

Darryl Williams

Darryl Williams

MY PRAYER

HOLINESS THANK YOU FOR MY BOUNDLESS BLESSINGS ALWAYS. PLEASE GIVE ME THE PIECE OF MIND THAT WILL ENABLE ME TO HAVE SERENITY WHEN EVIL APPEARS BOTH BIG AND SMALL. JESUS GIVE ME THE PATIENCE TO ALWAYS SEE THINGS THROUGH YOUR TIME FRAME AND NOT MY OWN. MASTER GIVE ME THE ABILITY TO ALWAYS PUT YOU FIRST IN ALL I DO. I KNOW I AM FIRST IN ALL THAT YOU DO FOR ME. LORD HELP ME TO GIVE TO SOMEONE ELSE A LITTLE OF WHAT YOU HAVE GIVEN ME. IN RETURN FOR YOUR GREATNESS I WILL TELL ALL THAT YOU HAVE GIVEN ME LIFE. YOU ARE MY ALPHA AND OMEGA AND THE ONLY FORCE IN MY UNIVERSE THAT HAS TO BE RECKONED WITN.

AMEN

Darryl Williams

BLADES OF GRASS

We all have things that we do that calms us, reduce stress or allow us to think. One activity that does all of these things for me is bike riding. When the weather is nice I usually ride my bike about a half a mile away from my home to where there are long wide-open roads with little traffic. I would ride on these roads until I reach the point where I would always turn around and come back home. I knew that there was a newly constructed bike, jogging, and roller blade path that ran along the edges of the shore adjacent to the highway that was just a couple of blocks away. Many times I had said to myself that I would go one day but I just never made an effort to go. The weather had gotten cold so I would have to wait until the spring until I could ride again.

Recently I took a short trip because I needed to get away because I needed some time alone away. I needed to be spiritually refreshed. During my trip I got a chance to get clear on a few things. One of those things was that I needed to make a little more time to do the things that I liked.

The very next day after I got back I got up early that morning. I put on my sweats and a jacket because the mornings were still just a little nippy. I got out my bike hopped on it and just rode. While I was riding I had remembered that shortly before I left for my trip the weather had started to break and I couldn't wait to ride my bike. I never did because every time I cleared a certain amount of time to go bike riding something or some one always needed my attention.

Darryl Williams

My first bike ride of the season was a symbol of the commitment to myself to have some time just for me. I rode past the point where I would usually turn around and come back home. I kept on riding while I was thinking and speaking to the spirit. The spirit lead me to the bike path that I never got a chance to go to before it had gotten cold. While on the path a bright white water bird suddenly appeared in the vegetation that ran along the shore. It looked as if it had just been bathed in milk because it was so white. As I approached the bird it was standing majestically upright and it did not move. It seemed as if it had been expecting me. The bird was a symbol of the spirit that lead me to this peaceful place.

Two days later I was on the bike path again this time I was with my boys. I was telling them about the bird I had seen before. Suddenly it appeared again. It was on wings and was just coming in for a landing in a clearing near us. The boys were amazed and excited at seeing the bird. We continued on with our ride and it was so peaceful. Later that day I meditated and prayed for healing and guidance. The next morning I got on my bike and rode along the shore again. I had been dealing with questions that I had about my role in this book.

The reasons why I had started this book in the first place months ago were reconfirmed again for me. I really felt the spiritual connection I needed to feel that allowed me to see why this book was so vital for me. I realized the magnitude of the messages that the spirit had chosen me to put on paper for all to read. The milky white bird that I saw on my rides along the shore was the spirit.

We are all very different people and come from as many different situations as there are blades of grass in the world. I do believe that there is in all of us the desire to be loved, appreciated, accepted, valued and nurtured, These desires are all there regardless of our character, personality and moral standards. Many of us have these desires met to a greater or lesser degrees depending on what our experiences have been.

I was not able to recognize the true importance of my own desires until I was able to start my own spiritual journey that would eventually lead me to understanding who and why I am. It is a journey that I am still on and will be on as long as I want to continue to experience the mystical magic that is the spirit with in.

I have had many experiences in my life. All of which have had a purpose. Some go back to the earliest memories I can remember as a child and some are as recent as a second just passed. When I think back on any of my experiences some make me smile or frown, laugh or cry, shut down or open up. Yet there are still others that would get a combination of any one. My experiences are unique to me in terms of their time, date, location, cause, affect, pain, joy and circumstances in which they occurred in my life. I know that my experiences are also universal to most if not all of you. All I have to do is take away the date, time, location, cause, effect, pain, joy and circumstances in which they occurred and my experiences are everyone's. If they are not yet then in time they will be.

Darryl Williams

THE HEART

All of the principals of life have a message. I have taken the heart of these messages and written them down so all can refer to them easily when needed.

The Flow - If you feel you are not going with the divine flow stop, pray and surrender.

Truth - Living in the truth will often mean dealing with things that have happened to us. Some of these things have defined who we are but the truth of these things never define who we will become.

Solitude/meditation - Replenish your spirit because on any given day you may be the only representation of the spirit that a person may experience at all.

Divine Order- Some times we have to step to the side so that divine order can flow.

Joy - When we use our God given talents we honor the spirit and show that we are thankful for our blessings.

Faith - Your faith can only be based on your own lessons in life.

Wisdom - Wisdom is not something that comes with age. It can come at anytime.

Patience - Many of life lessons will have to be repeated until they are learned.

Acceptance - Accept people for who and what they are not who you want them to be.

Humor - A gift from the divine that when used show our gratitude.

Freedom - True freedom only comes after you know that the spirit is who you are.

Courage - Courage decides if you sit on the sidelines or become an active participant in your life.

Gratitude - Gratitude opens the door to our soul and creates a place for the spirit to dwell.

Non-judgment - Non- judgment is easy to understand but hard to implement in to our lives.

Forgiveness - Forgiveness is something that all should do but forgetting waste precious time, energy and spirit.

Compassion - Compassion allows us to spend our time enjoying our lessons/blessing not repeating them.

ABOUT THE AUTHOR

Darryl Williams has been writing for a few years now. He has a written several short stories, essays and poems. His poetry is being compiled and should be complete soon.

Mr. Williams holds degrees from Brooklyn College and Certificates from New York State Office of Children and Family Services and SUNY Early Childhood Education. He is the founder of a Small Not- For- Profit Day Care.

Mr. Williams lives with his two sons whom he has been raising with the help and support of a loving family for the past seven years. Mr. Williams enjoys writing, reading, spending time with loved ones and enjoying his blessing. DIVINE EESSYS FROM THE SPIRIT WITHIN is his first published work. He is now currently working on his first novel.